Favorite CLASSICAL Melodies

TROMBONE

Arranged and Recorded by David Pearl
("Brandenburg Concerto No. 5, First Movement" arranged and recorded by Donald Sosin)

Cherry Lane Music Company
Director of Publications/Project Supervisor: Mark Phillips

ISBN: 978-1-60378-416-0

Visit our website at www.cherrylaneprint.com

CONTENTS

AVE MARIA

TROMBONE

By Charles Gounod and Johann Sebastian Bach

Moderately slow

Piano

BRANDENBURG CONCERTO NO. 5,
FIRST MOVEMENT

By Johann Sebastian Bach

TROMBONE

Adagietto

CARO MIO BEN

TROMBONE

By Giuseppe Giordani

Moderately slow
Orchestra

CLAIR DE LUNE

TROMBONE

By Claude Debussy

Slowly

cresc.

poco rit.   *mf*   *p*

FUNERAL MARCH OF A MARIONETTE

TROMBONE

by Charles Gounod

Moderately fast, in 2

GYMNOPÉDIE NO. 1

TRACK 6

TROMBONE

By Erik Satie

Moderately

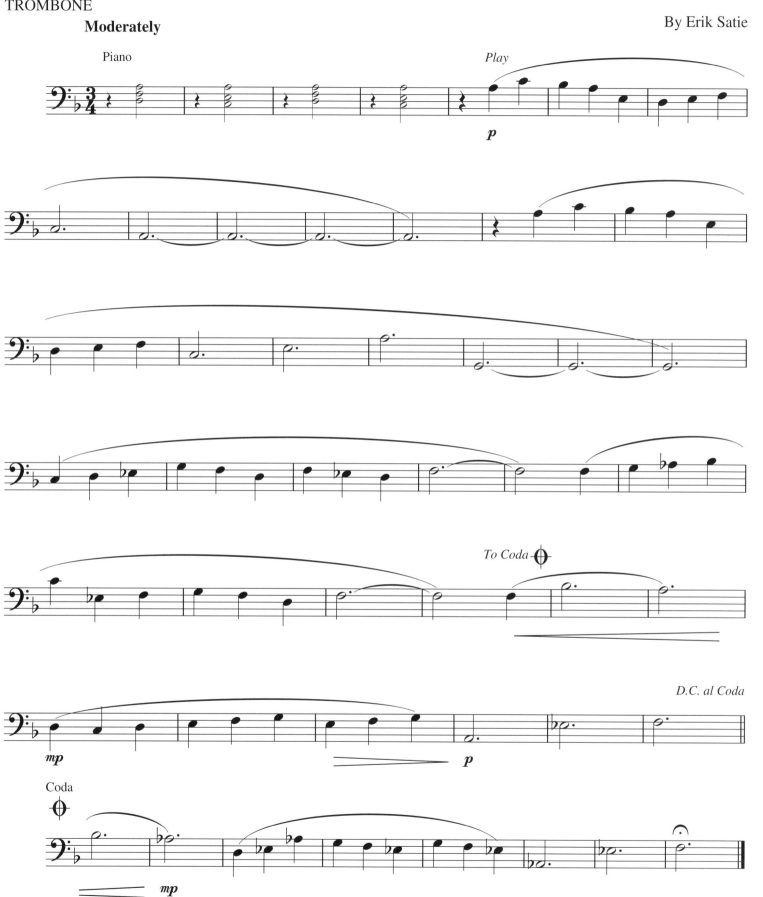

HALLELUJAH CHORUS

from *Messiah*

By George Frideric Handel

TROMBONE

Moderately fast

Piano

HUNGARIAN DANCE NO. 5

TROMBONE

By Johannes Brahms

Moderately

Slower

Tempo I

MINUET
(from String Quintet in E Major)

By Luigi Boccherini

TROMBONE

Moderately

PIANO SONATA NO. 14 "MOONLIGHT"

First Movement

TROMBONE

By Ludwig van Beethoven

SYMPHONY NO. 5

First Movement

TROMBONE

By Ludwig van Beethoven

Moderately fast

Orchestra

WILLIAM TELL OVERTURE

TROMBONE

By Gioacchino Rossini

Moderately fast

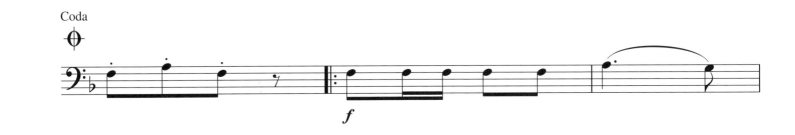

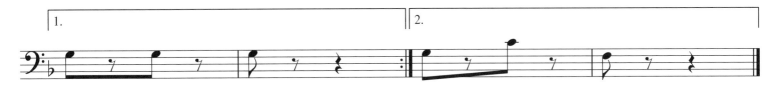

POMP AND CIRCUMSTANCE

TROMBONE

By Edward Elgar